Introduction

As the centenary of the birth of G...,
and translator, in August 1904 approaches, we, his
daughters, believe that this should be marked by a celebration of Gwyn's lifelong attachment to Mynydd
Bach in Ceredigion. This journal of a summer spent in
Trefenter dates back more than half a century to a time
when he began to gain recognition as a translator and
critic and for his own poetry and drama. Against the
background of the wide range of his writings in many
genres the journal seems to distil into a short piece
Gwyn's links and commitment to his ancestral and
spiritual home.

Gwyn traced his Mynydd Bach ancestors on his
father's side back to 1700, and believed he had made
his first visit to Mynydd Bach before he was born,
when his father took his Glamorgan-born mother to
meet relatives and see his home village in the first year
of their marriage. During his childhood, the family
spent summer holidays staying at Minffordd, the home
of his father's aunt, Bodo Martha. From then onwards
he spent as much of each summer there as possible,
with a break only during the Second World War when
he was unable to return from Egypt. After the war he
met Daisy in Alexandria; he took her to Mynydd Bach
for the first time in the summer of 1948, they married in
1949 at the end of a summer spent there and they
returned for the following two summers. Later they
were to spend a number of years in the 1950s and fif-
teen years of Gwyn's retirement living in Trefenter.

Gwyn's 1951 summer journal portrays a way of life
which was a unique mix of rural, literary and artistic

pursuits: helping with the hay harvest and sheep shearing, taking long walks across the mountain, swimming in the lake, shooting, sketching, writing, visiting the National Library to research and translate Welsh poetry. They were often joined by Gwyn's sons, David and Ifan, our half-brothers. While Gwyn wrote his account Daisy collected a scrapbook of drawings, photographs and newspaper cuttings which illustrated their summer. Although they did not realise it at the time, 1951 was to be the last such summer and in retrospect this journal becomes a snapshot of a vanished life.

Teleri Williams and Lowri Gwilym

Contents

List of illustrations

Summer Journal 1951

Gwyn Williams

Planet

First published
in Wales in 2004
by Planet

PO Box 44
Aberystwyth
Ceredigion SY23 3ZZ
Cymru/Wales

Design: Glyn Rees

Cover image: *Harvest, Mynydd Bach* by Daisy Williams

Printed by Gwasg Gomer
Llandysul, Ceredigion

ISBN: 0 9540881 2 3

Summer Journal
1951

Prologue

Atgofion Mynydd Bach

Dod i Drefenter cartre fy Nhad am fis yn yr haf o'r Sowth, o Sir Forganwg, oedd uchafbwynt y flwyddyn i mi fel plentyn. Dod ar y trên i Dregaron, Strata Florida neu Lanilar — y fan un-ceffyl yn ein disgwyl, codi o'r cymoedd i awyr y mynydd ac anadlu gwynt mwg y tanau mawn yn codi o'r tyddynod twt. Rwy'n dal i dorri mawn ar y comin — mae mawnen ar y tân nawr — ond yn fwy na defnydd tân mae mawn i mi'n fath o arogldarth sy'n ail-greu Trefenter fy mebyd. Mawn i'w losgi, y plant yn siarad Cymraeg a'r tyddynod bach yn cadw i fynd — dyna'r pethe pwysig i mi yma.

Memories of Mynydd Bach

Coming to Trefenter, my father's home, for a month in the summer, up from the South, from Glamorganshire, was the highlight of my year as a child. We would come up by train to Tregaron, Strata Florida or Llanilar and the one-horse van would be waiting for us. As it took us up from the valleys to the mountain air we'd smell the smoke of the peat fires rising from the tidy little cottages. I still cut peat on the common — there's a lump of peat on the fire now — but more than a fuel, peat to me is a kind of aroma that recreates the Trefenter of my childhood. Peat to burn, the children speaking Welsh and the smallholdings keeping going — those are the important things for me here.

Gwyn Williams

Summer Journal

Friday 29th June 1951

Got to Blaenbeidog at 10.15 a.m. from Lampeter by David Dan Richards' little lorry. Auntie Mary lighting the fire, so we got clothes out to air. A fine hot day. Spent the afternoon laying in the potato field, with David and Llwyd the pony scuffling and ploughing back the earth. After tea planted mustard, cress, lettuce and six weeks turnips in a half-row at the bottom of the field. Daisy found a yellow hammer's nest with a sitting bird in a blackberry bush. Watered our seeds after supper. Went up to Cors Pwll yr Ych before dark to see the peat David has cut and were horrified by the number of black-headed gulls breeding there. Daisy estimated five hundred in the air.

Saturday 30th June

Up at 7.30. After bacon and eggs and coffee borrowed sickle, spade and pickaxe at Tangraig and set about digging the first sanitary hole in the garden. Then cleaned nettles away from the path and gate to the house. Llyn Eiddwen in the afternoon and swam twice, the water not cold once one got under. Picked up a lot of wool the sheep are casting to make a cushion. After tea down to Tynant for wood and brought a good bundle home each. Rabbit in casserole with onions, herbs and bacon for supper.

It was excellent.

Sunday 1st July

Spent the morning clearing old books and papers out of the chest and burning them. David started to get the boat ready for extensive repairs. Layed about until early tea with a little excitement when the Gorslwyd men came to borrow Dai's trap and backed it into our hedge. After tea Daisy and I went up to the lake and I swam and washed myself and Juby, who enjoyed it. On the way over Hafod Ithel Juby started to dig into a rabbit hole and wouldn't come away. We left her and had to come back and I noticed a wheatear hovering above. Juby snarled and snapped when I tried to pull her out and then she pulled out a nest with four fledglings which she quickly crushed. We went away feeling very angry with her.

Gathered wool for our cushion. The sheep are casting their wool everywhere and it's shearing time this week.

A thick mist had come up by nine o'clock (I told Dai it would reach us from the sea before dark) and Dai is still out rounding sheep for tomorrow's washing. It's impossible to see a sheep at more than fifty yards.

Monday 2nd July

Cut nettles around house in morning. To Aber at one — bus from Troedfoel. Big shopping. Jack Edwards have sold out *The Rent* [*The Rent That's Due to Love*, Editions Poetry London, 1950]. David and Uncle Dan brought us a load of hay home. Daisy did a great cooking in the morning, a very good cake, gooseberry roll, egg and bacon pie and a gooseberry pie. I stuffed and roasted a rabbit. All excellent eating.

Tuesday 3rd July

Ifan says he expects to come about August 4th, writing from Lowestoft.

Daisy did a wash and cleared out accumulated rubbish whilst I took out the sink lead pipe and fitted it back to run into a bucket instead of into the ground through the wall. It was blocked anyhow. In the afternoon put the hay together into cocks at Cae Crugiau. Dai Morus away at the Fron Fynwent shearing. After tea Daisy and I dug part of the field to put down cabbage plants I bought at Aber. Hard work — the earth full of huge stones. The lettuce and turnips we planted on Friday are showing their heads.

Before supper put on our wellingtons to go into Cors Pwll yr Ych to look at the black-headed gulls breeding there. Saw young birds in the air, some doing their first twenty-yard flights, a lot of strong runners, one nest with three fluffy chicks which squeaked heartily when picked up, a nest with two and another with one egg. Put up four snipe.

Wednesday 4th July

Uncle Dan helped me to put down the cabbage in the morning. In the afternoon went over to Llwynrhyddod to contemplate the house and collect firewood.

Thursday 5th July

Mended Daisy's shoe in the morning. In the afternoon went over to the lake and swam. Mari Waungron called on her way to Bancllyn. She's eighty-six and complains that she can't get one leg to go faster than the other. Did the chimney too this morning (the parlour chimney) with David on top thumping and me pulling and pushing from below. Thick wads of jackdaw nests came down after an hour of this and we lit a fire there. No fungus yet except an excellent puffball some days ago.

Friday 6th July

A great walk. Set out after lunch across the mountain to Lledrod. Thence up to the Gaer Fawr (with a double back of over a mile to pick up a pullover I idiotically dropped and which Daisy ran to earth at Ty'n yr Helyg, where a woman had picked it up at a stile. Bought oranges (6d each) at Lledrod. Greatly impressed by the vast earthworks of Y Gaer and the splendid all round view. Decided not to risk going to Trawscoed but to cut across country to Llanilar, which we did with great success via Llety Moel, Ty'n yr Eithin, Ty'n Berllan and Castle Hill. A couple of bottles of Bass at the Falcon and, having been refused bread and cheese (dreadful state for a country to be in), got biscuits and potato crisps at Morris' shop. Caught the bus to Bronant and home over the mountain. Altogether well over twelve miles.

Saw extraordinary flowers, thousands of orchises, spotted and butterfly, and an as yet identified dark red one.* Great patches of a yellow flower Daisy identifies as Dyer's Greenweed in amongst bracken, and at Lledrod a Jersey Cudweed, which I'd never seen before. The foxgloves and wild roses were lovely and the honeysuckle opening everywhere.

At Ty'n yr Eithin we talked to a young red-haired Englishman who's bought the farm from Llidiardau and lived there for eighteen months without a road to his house except a right of way through fields. He was glad to talk to anyone and offered us a cup of tea but we had to get on.

Saturday 7th July

Great preparations at Tangraig and Pant Amlwg for the shearing. Spent most of the afternoon sheltering from

*This may be the Fragrant Orchis.

rain under the *gambo* in which Dai Morus was carrying rushes. David dressed up and went to town.

Sunday 8th July

David worked on the boat in the morning with stuff he brought from town and I fixed the pipe to the sink with putty. In the afternoon Daisy and I went to the lake and swam between showers. Sheltered at Tanbwlch on the way back and drank our thermos of tea and ate excellent mincemeat tart that Daisy made this morning. She baked a very good looking cake too as well as other things, a pie and a treacle tart. David and I had stewed beef for lunch which I had too liberally treated with chillies.

David is working on our bikes so any day may find us whipping off to the coast for a swim.

Auntie Mary is reading *Cyflawnder Bendith* [The Fullness of Grace], a dozen copies of which I remember the author giving my father to sell when I was a boy. I have given them *The Rent* but they've made no comment yet. Rather a spiced meal for chapel-goers perhaps.

Daisy made pancakes after supper and we invited Dai Morus in to share.

Monday 9th July

Sheepshearing, with thirteen shearers and half a dozen carriers, David and I amongst them. It all went well, but with rather less leg-pulling than I expected. Daisy sketched the shearers and helped with tea at Tangraig. We're all tired and go early to bed.

Heard about the illness of old John Edwards the retired minister at Llangwyryfon. For weeks during last winter he insisted on having two watchers with him during the night. Trefenter offered few volunteers and even Llangwyryfon got tired of him. His bed was made up in the living room and he went to it dressed in his tail coat and white stock and, some say, with his umbrella. One night when his housekeeper was afraid to go out in the dark to get a watcher he offered to go with her. He got up every day.

Juby's bite looks bad. I've cleaned it several times with Dettol but the flesh seems to have mortified around a nasty black hole. Dai Morus gave me some blue stone (copper sulphate I think) and I made a solution and poured it over the wound. At Tangraig and Pant Amlwg they take the usual philosophical attitude. They've seen worse, it may get better or it may finish her. We are more deeply concerned. Dan Fronfynwent, who judges dogs, said that carbolic and green oil was the stuff and I'm going to try to get it at Lampeter tomorrow.

Tuesday 10th July

Went off between showers to catch the mart bus to Lampeter at Moriah, the bus half an hour late. A big mart but not very interesting, mostly cows with calf and piglets, milk and bacon being the profit-makers. Daisy spent a good part of the day at Rhys Hughes', the sale having started that morning, and got a good cheap mack and collected her new coat, whilst I picked up some good sub-standard wool socks and bought a good raincoat to take back with me. In the evening phoned Jack Lloyd Jones and arranged to meet him and his wife at 8.30 at the Troed y Rhiw. Sat happily drinking and telling stories in the parlour until 10.30, whilst the wireless bellowed out the Robinson-Turpin fight in another part of the pub. Jack told a good story about the Lampeter borough surveyor. Emrys Jones and a friend were sitting talking about someone they hadn't had news of for a long time and the surveyor butted in with the information, "Oh, he's been at Rigor Mortis for years now." He meant Bognor Regis.

When we got home Megan and Maldwyn were up, Maldwyn tuned in to the end of the fight, and he told us a story about a mad woman we'd seen a fortnight ago, and who has avoided locking up by always contriving to be out when the medical officer calls. Her husband died and Davies the undertaker in doing the job left a new overcoat he was wearing in the parlour. He went out for an hour or so and when he came back failed to find his coat until he found that it was on the body in the coffin.

Bought a few more small things on Wednesday morning and left by bus for Bronant in the afternoon. Were lucky, after the downpour of the morning, not to get wet walking over the mountain.

Thursday 12th July

Daisy did a big wash whilst I pottered. I cooked the rabbit David shot yesterday. After lunch we set out for Bronant to test our bicycles and get the week's rations. Daisy's brakes gave out soon after Bryncewyll and she went whizzing by me. I thought it was a joke and speeded up a bit to catch her and was surprised to see her jump off on a more level bit of road. Her bike had been completely out of control. David had put one new brake block on the back wheel instead of two, the other was worn flat and the brake didn't engage. So she had to walk down hill as well as up, that is most of the way to Bronant and back. I put on a new block to make a pair tonight and fixed her seat which had been cocking up embarassingly.

David is making preparations for his ride to Southport tomorrow.

I think Juby's wound is better and she is very lively today. I got some carbolised green oil at Lampeter and it seems to be having an effect.

The black-headed gulls are coming in to the sheep fold again tonight. When I went out after dark a few nights ago they rose in hundreds absolutely silently so that the lighter sky to the west was half obscured by birds' wings with no sound at all, not a single cry. The sheep didn't stir, obviously being used to them. We haven't been to see the chicks in Pwll yr Ych since.

Friday 13th July

A very cold day. Picked three pounds of billberries down Lôn Sais in the morning and made two and a half pounds of jam in the evening. Worked on the hay in Cae Crugiau in the afternoon.

Saturday 14th July

Set off at two o'clock on our bicycles for Llanon. Swam and had tea on the shingle. Sketched the church. Saw oyster-catchers and cormorants fishing. Back through

Llanrhystyd for a pint of beer and home slowly up Cwm Mabws. Supper of beef sausages bought at Llanon.

Sunday 15th July

Daisy and I both tired after yesterday and I with a headache brought on by glare of road and shingle, I think. Followed Dai Morus up to Blaenwyre in the

morning and whilst he talked to the Penglanwen boys I found a pigeon's nest and a brown owl's at Lluest Lâs. The owl flew to a nearby tree and stared at me.

Took an unashamed siesta in the afternoon and after tea went up to the bog. Got the telescope on the black-headed gull nests and laughed at the ridiculous behaviour of the immature gulls bowing and squawking at each other. Surprised to see a plover (I think golden) among them. A teal got up and flew to a patch of water not two hundred yards away and she made a perfect picture in the telescope, sitting motionless on the water with an eye towards us. I got Dai Morus to put her up and was astonished at the great spring she made into the air before flattening out into her flight.

After supper went up to Blaenwyre again with Daisy, Dai Morus and Juby, taking the telescope. Counted the sheep there (134) and admired the great leaps of a strong two-year-old black ewe as she went through the counting gap.

Monday 16th July

Went to Aberystwyth, shopped and phoned the Gwyn Joneses. Met Tom Jones and a Harvard professor of Celtic who is at Aber to learn the pronunciation of Welsh. Lunched off our own sandwiches and beer at the very pleasantly redecorated Farmers Arms and then to the beach where Gwyn Jones joined us and afterwards Alice. Borrowed *Cerdd Dafod* [by Sir John Morris-Jones, the rules of *cynghanedd* and strict-metre poetry] from Tom Jones. Back to Troedfoel on the bus. An excellent supper of mackerel. A lovely sunset and a yellow full moon suggest that we may be in for a spell of fine weather.

Must one day explore the bosky, untravelled, secret Wyre valley from Llangwyryfon to the sea.

Tuesday 17th July

Daisy baked this morning and sewed all afternoon and evening. Her new grey coat looked very good yesterday.

I spent the day in the hay fields and made five loads this afternoon. Apropos of the muddle some of our acquaintances have made of BBC news and weather reports, Dai Morus told me a story of Huw Pantybarwn coming to meet him excitedly on Banc Tynant last Christmas time saying, "Have you heard what the wireless says? The King of England's lost his crown." "Good God!" says Dai. "What was the matter? Was he drunk?" It seems that Huw's wife hadn't understood the report of the brave carrying off of the Stone of Scone.

Daisy and I went to Bryngwartheg field and found a number of fresh puffballs to fry for breakfast tomorrow. No mushrooms yet nor any sign of the delicious chanterelles we had in profusion some summers ago.

Juby's cut has dried up completely and this morning she had two good runs after rabbits she put up off the Llwynrhyddod field.

Sparrows have nested in the roof beams of Pant

Amlwg hayshed and I watched them whilst making the stack and noticed that the parent birds were bringing in huge lumps of what looked like chicken food. We found Auntie Mary feeding the chickens and ducks when we passed the front of the house. So pressing was the need to get the food to the squawking chicks that the parent birds took little notice of me.

Wednesday 18th July

Sent off £35, three years' arrears of National Insurance Fund, to start my contributions and finished my letter of comment to Terence Tiller on his *cynghanedd* in English. Began to put together my appendix on Welsh versification [for *Introduction to Welsh Poetry*, Faber & Faber, 1953].

In the afternoon gathered gorse wood with Daisy and played hide and seek with a pair of stoats in the stone wall of Banc Tynant — Caeau Meica. This evening left Daisy, who couldn't leave her cooking vegetables, and went up to Blaenwyre with Dai Morus to look at the sheep. All well except that one of the pet lambs has disappeared. The other we found alone in an abandoned house.

Between us we did a piece of detective work on a few feathers and some droppings in a little quarry. On a ledge under the top run of turf we found bird droppings, four kestrel feathers, two flight, one back and one breast, and alongside some dung which Dai Morus said was fox. At first we thought the kestrel had perched there and preened its feathers, then that the fox had caught a kestrel and carried it there. But I looked at the flight feathers and found them both broken off at exactly the same place about two inches from the end, so that it looked as though the fox had snapped and got only a few feathers. The fox had rounded quite a snug resting place for himself on the ledge.

Back to find Daisy doing research in preparation for our Port Talbot trip next week, looking up maps and antiquarian stuff. I see plans of Margam Abbey across the table.

Extraordinary effects of mist on the mountain tonight. It would close in suddenly so that visibility was about fifty yards, sheep would look like llamas and cows like eagles. Then it would clear in one direction and some two or three miles away we would see a sweep of sunlit green and yellow fields, unbelievably light and bright.

Thursday 19th July

Got as far as the *englyn cyrch* in my notes on Welsh prosody this morning. The wind has been north to north-west, so that the gunnery or bombing or whatever murderous childishness they're up to in North Wales thumped all the morning. How it makes me hate all soldiery and the idea of England. The Irish manage without this daily violation of their peaceful soil. Or if they have violence there's a local meaning to it. This is the worst occupation we have suffered here in over two thousand years. It threatens from all sides, through War Office, Forestry Commission, Butlin camp, National Park play grounds for Birmingham, Reservoirs and electrical schemes. Perhaps a few Welsh black cattle and a ram or so will be kept to give atmosphere. *Yn boeth y bo'r diawlaid* [May the Devil take them].

Went up to the lake after lunch, swam and bathed Juby who is very lively now her wound is better. She came back flour-white.

After an early tea (three o'clock) went to help Dai Morus with the hay and made six loads whilst he and Morris Llain pitched. Worked till 9.30 so that Daisy was bad-tempered, a rare thing, thinking I'd been gossiping with Dai.

A beautiful evening and at ten the patches of ground mist made queer effects with rocks and trees.

Reading Camus' *La Peste* (in translation) a few pages a night makes me feel that call at Oran every day to see how the plague's getting on.

Friday 20th July

To Aberystwyth. Put in an hour and a half at the library on Einion Offeiriad's rules for poetry. Tremendous lunch at Gwyn Jones' where we met a Miss Griffin, an American mediaeval historian, who's working on a history of the Mortimers in Wales. Swam after lunch. Walked up from Lôn Sais.

Saturday 21st July

Got the oven going for Daisy to bake and went to Lôn Sais to pick billberries. Back to find Tommy, Enid, the three boys and my mother had arrived. Lunch took some time and then to the lake. Tommy shot a mallard with my gun. Mam wouldn't leave the car because of the Bancllyn bull. Took Tommy and the boys to Pwll yr Ych after tea to show them the black-headed gull colony. The birds had left the nest where Daisy and I saw them as chicks a fortnight ago but there was a dead mouse in the next. Several explanations put forward. I saw the lone plover (peewit) rise with the gulls so it must have been reared with them. I saw it through the telescope walking about with young gulls last week. Another mystery.

After the Llangrannog people left I went back to Pwll yr Ych to look for teal or snipe. I trudged over nearly all the bog and at last got a shot at a snipe which I got with the first barrel. Nothing else rose except gulls, which must keep everything away with their screeching and their stink. Brian Vesey Fitzgerald says they suck the eggs of other birds too, and they're certainly driving away the ravens that have nested for years in a willow in the middle of the bog.

Sunday 22nd July

Full of an awful cold I caught sweating and cooling on Friday. Have worked off and on all day at my appendix on metrics. Dai Morus greatly concerned at a threatened inspection of his sheep since he may not have the right numbers in the right places. He has had a good deal to say today about officials and forms as a result.

Auntie Mary brought us our first mushroom. Today's thunderstorm should bring up some more. David is expected back tomorrow from his stay with Ieuan and at Southport. The peat he cut is serving us well and I'm going to keep the fire in tonight in case it's wet to go out for sticks in the morning.

About two thirds of the gulls have left Cors Pwll yr Ych. Gone down to the promenades in time for Bank Holiday probably. The curlew are assembling too. We have greenfinches nesting near the house and a wren in the pigsty.

Monday 23rd July

Gwyn and Alice Jones to lunch and tea. Gwyn talked about Iceland, which interested Dai Morus, particularly the ponies. How difficult it is for the intelligent town-dweller to avoid a patronising attitude towards the countryman.

Friday 24th July

Left Blaenbeidog at 9.30 for Port Talbot via the mountain, bus to Lampeter (lunch at Megan's) and so to P.T. Went out to Margam in the evening and was delighted to find a great deal of beauty there though its secrecy is gone with the denuding of the hills of the old oaks. Got the key of the museum and spent some time with the assembled stones, Bodvoe, Pumperiius Carantorious and the Celtic crosses. A gargoyle indecently proportioned delighted Daisy. It is refreshing that such a joke in stone should not be hidden away somewhere. One up to the Office of Works. Walked up to the chapel on the hill and saw two deer leap over the four-foot fence of the afforestation area. They are the wild remnants of the old park herd and it was good to see them behave wildly.

Wednesday 25th July

Saw the book exhibition at the Taibach library in the morning — rather too incomplete a record of local history. The *Annales de Margam* from Trinity, Cambridge outstanding.

Bus to Porthcawl after lunch. Tea there. Then out to Rest Bay where I swam, Daisy sketched and I collected winkles. On to Sker and spent some time looking at the grim Sker House and its mediaeval barns. Walked over dunes to Mawdlam, looked at the pool with the building standing out of the water and unsuccessfully for the remains of the city of Cynffig. A drink at the Angel (we missed the Prince of Wales somehow) which rocked with song from an Aberavon bus party finishing off a day in good style. Then bus home.

Thursday 26th July

To Cardiff in the morning by bus. The Castle before lunch — extraordinary mixture of mediaeval and Victorian opulence. The guide suitably lighthearted. In the dining room he indicated concealed bells, one, an acorn held by a monkey, for the servant, the other, more concealed, for the wife; and when rung, "up she came a-running". Interested to see Jasper Tudor's additions after reading poems in his honour.

A quick visit to the Museum for the pre-historic stuff and particularly pleased to see the urn from Garn Wen where Daisy and I dug last year. A good and refreshing collection of work by young Welsh painters. Petts' picture of colliers stood out well. A good show of Richard Wilsons.

After lunch at Howell's pleasant Orchid Room went out to St Fagan's. Pleasantly impressed. Excellent pictures in the house — a gem of a Mark Gheraarts. Watched the wood-turner and bought a pretty little red bowl in medlar work. Then to the crafts exhibition. Bought Ewenny jugs and tankard and arranged to have a coracle made at Cenarth.

Walked through the docks (using ferry) to lock gates, watched a ship bunkering. Then to Aberavon beach which looked rather bleak for the busloads of women and children arriving at midday. The buses came from Cardiff and there were several black women with children amongst them. Wondered how long the new houses will withstand the shifting sandhills. Another buried city like Cenffyg probably. On the way back got off the bus to look for the old Town Hall at Green Park Aberavon but were told that it fell down years ago. When I saw it last it had a roof on it and was being used by a rag and bone merchant. The only good building in Aberavon and Port Talbot gone and no one to regret it. Twll yn y Wal is doomed too and I've promised to write a letter about it.

Afternoon went to Margam, sketched and then were told by a mason to ask the head gardener to let us in to the grounds. He rather grudgingly (and quite rightly) agreed, so we spent an hour in and about ruins and orangery. Very gratifying to be able to show them to Daisy.

In the evening with Dilys and Stan for a tour of the steelworks (Port Talbot). Daisy got suitably frightened. We must paint there some day and about the docks. Stan told us that not a scrap of all the railings etc. collected during the war was used to make steel. The content of metal was insufficient and alloys corroded the bricking of the furnaces so that they had to be remade and time and money lost. They knew this but no one in the government asked them.

We followed the whole process from melting shop to bar mill with cranes and chargers swinging, noiseless in the clangour, about our heads. I had a feeling of immense forces fighting to get loose, flames forcing their way out of furnace doors, huge red hot bars bouncing on the rollers, steam hissing out of the ground, a chained force not quite under control. Stan walked through it, however, with the confidence of a ballet dancer.

We were glad of a drink at the Grand — immense pub — after. Two nights before I'd gone in there with Stan and helped a Norwegian or Dutchman whose only English word was porter. The young barmaid had never heard of porter, so recommended stout after a considerable triangular exchange of words bottle, porter and stout, with gestures. The Dutchman and his fellow sailor drank the stout without saying a word to each other and went out. Down in Aberavon they would get on better.

Saturday 28th July

To Lampeter by bus. A quiet afternoon and then after tea to the Eisteddfod, where we stayed till midnight with excursions for supper and a drink. The harpist's not turning up was a disappointment and the *penillion* had to be sung to the piano. The male voice choirs sang as well as it is possible for men to sing, particularly the Beaufort, Tredegar and Ystradgynlais choirs. The last named won, singing Joseph Parry's "Iesu o Nasareth" [Jesus of Nazareth]. Tredegar sang an Elgar which we didn't like. We watched the keenness with which they all listened to the adjudication afterwards and the sporting way the Tredegar men clapped the Ystradgynlais victory.

We were greatly entertained by the comic and serious recitations for grown ups too.

Sunday 29th July

A quiet day. Wrote a letter to the *Port Talbot Guardian* about Twll yn y Wal [Hole in the Wall] and antiquity in general. Walked along the Teifi in the afternoon and picked flowers which Daisy arranged greatly to Mam's delight.

Monday 30th July

Took Rhys by bus to New Quay on a hot day. Lunched on the beach and swam several times. Rhys enjoyed himself and was no trouble until the return journey when growing proximity to home made him more disobedient. Daisy built him an effective sand castle.

In the evening went to the Welsh drama night at which Maldwyn was chairman. Three one-act plays, all by Cardiganshire writers, notably Idwal Jones (*P'un?*). Impressed by the frankness and realism of the two tragic plays and their avoidance of any possible happy ending. The heroine of one brought up an illegitimate child who in turn fell in love with her first cousin unbeknownst. Out of this something considerable may come in Wales.

I gave Daisy an occasional explanation and she enjoyed the evening.

Thursday 31st July

Tommy brought us to Tregaron where David, the girls and Dai Morus were to meet us. Met a number of old acquaintances, lunched (not very well) at the Talbot and then went to see the exhibition of local history at the new school, taking with us quite a party including Morris Llain and Jack Nant yr Hwch and his brother. Some gratification at our appearance and we were all introduced to the vicar and the headmaster, a Jesus [College] man. An extremely good show of local things, documents, implements, quilts, objects from Strata Florida and tumuli, flints etc.

Went shooting with Dai Morus and Daisy after supper to Garn Wen and got a curlew. Dai got two curlews and a mallard and we both missed several in the deepening twilight.

Wednesday 1st August

Made a shelf with brass hooks for plates and jugs this morning.

Thursday 2nd August

A quiet day at home. I carried two dead trees home with Daisy's help from Tanfoel. David got two loads of peat, and we all threw them in.

Friday 3rd August

Went off early to Aber to meet Daisy's mother. Wondered whether David and the girls would really go camping in the threatening weather. Spent an hour and a half at the library copying specimens of the twenty-four measures [of Welsh poetry]. Sandwich lunch with Daisy at the Farmers Arms. Morris Llain brought us all up in his car.

Saturday 4th August

Helped Dai Morus with some rough hay and went shooting with him after supper. We did the usual pools and bits of bog and put nothing up. Dai got a teal at a pool beyond Garn Wen but the mountain was very quiet. The curlew seem to have gone. A lovely evening with a wild sky. The sky cleared after dark and on the way home we saw a flying saucer, or what has come to be called so. It was fairly high in a clear patch of sky to the north-west, lying at an angle of about twenty-five degrees to the horizon and of a length in the sky roughly equal to the distance between the two bottom stars in the coulter of the Plough. It shone like polished silver, was very slim and slightly curved on the top side. It was extremely bright when I first looked up at it and pointed it out to Dai. As he looked it got paler and in about two seconds later it had vanished. It gave me the impression of being extremely far away, but it was quite distinct in the sky.

Sunday 5th August

Talked to Ifan over the phone. He's coming up tomorrow or Tuesday.

Finished my treatment of the 24 measures and *cynghanedd*. Only a note on rhyme now to finish the appendix.

Daisy's mother has been happy picking whinberries and making jam.

Went to Blaenwyre with Daisy, Dai and a hundred sheep. Caught the stray pet lambs in Penglanwen field and brought them back to Bryngwartheg. They are afraid of nothing and when the gander attacked them at Llwynrhyddod they just looked at him. He pulled out a mouthful of wool and then got them by the nose, but they seemed to like it and he was very taken aback. But Carlo kept far enough away from them.

Monday 6th August

Dug a splendid hole in the corner of the garden this morning and made a three cornered stool in the afternoon. Daisy's mother has picked a lot of whinberries and made two pounds of jam. This evening unless it rains Dai Morus and I are going to Llanrhystud for a few pints of beer. It was once our practice to go to Aberystwyth on Bank Holiday Monday but we haven't done that for some years.

Tuesday 7th August

We got down to Llanrhystud very quickly on our bicycles and put them into the garage of the Red Lion.

There was good company there, Stephen Rhosgoch, who once worked for my father, Siami Ystrad Teilo, Dan y Felin, etc., and Dai was soon in excellent reminiscent fettle.

Note: Redness in N.E. sky gave me notion of story — England burning, the cattle escape along green roads. X Remember the corpse and the overcoat story.

Someone in the parlour was playing the piano and a violin and there was cheerful singing. A tenor sang "Jerusalem". We drank four pints of beer and then just about stop tap two bottles of Bass each. Then just as we were going out Dai Morus saw someone who had just got married and got a whisky each for us out of him. It's the custom at Llanrhystud for anyone who gets married to give the publican a few pounds to serve drinks to familiars at his discretion. Outside there was the usual political discussion in which I sided with Dai's Welsh Nationalism, though insisting on a left-wing view.

Dai was in no hurry to start off and in no state to cycle much. Davies Gorslwyd had promised to bring his van back to meet us along the road and this gave Dai an excuse for dawdling to get a longer ride. So we took a long time to get up Rhiwbwys having had to walk out of the village with our lampless bikes. It was dark when we got to a flat piece of road and we went off madly until Dai either fell or jumped off on recognising a crossroad. I just managed to pull up against his bike which was lying in the middle of the road and the sudden braking pulled the brake block across the spokes. I took it to the hedge and, having failed to push it back, got the nut off with my fingers. I'd had it off a fortnight before so it came off easily.

Dai Morus remarks: — What I can't understand is

why, since the English are such liars, they ever believe each other.

By this time we had given Davies up and were faced with a five mile walk in the dark. It was now so dark that we couldn't see turnings and only barely see the road. At Rhyd Rhosser the rain came and we huddled in a hedge under trees. I couldn't see Dai and I think he went to sleep. I've no idea how long we were there, but I was on the point of abandoning myself to a soaking when the rain lightened and we went on. Dai wanted to stay there and sleep it out. It was completely dark now and we couldn't see each other whilst walking side by side. I tried the experiment of walking with eyes shut and found it made no difference. One's feet told one whether one was on the centre of the road, the gravelly side or the grass border. Several times I had one leg in the ditch. At one point Dai said he couldn't push the bike at all and threatened to throw it over the hedge. I felt it all over (Dai's matches were finished as a result of examining my brake block) and found the front wheel jammed against the frame. It took me a little while to realise that he had turned the handlebars completely round in jacking the bike up. Later his chain came off and I put that back. He hated the bike so much by this time that he would hardly push it. He quoted Bernard Shaw's remark that man thought the bicycle was his servant whereas the reverse was true.

Near the Moriah — Llangwyryfon road it lightened a little and we could vaguely see the road. I tried free-wheeling on the pedal from the top of the hill down to Lôn Sais, but couldn't keep out of the hedge. The beer had something to do with this. Halfway up Lôn Sais the blackness closed in again and I failed to find the turning up to Bryn Amlwg though I knew I was at it and could see the vague outline of trees. I pushed my wheel twice into the ditch and Dai shouted behind me, "Take the higher turning, it's easier." This I found by going straight on until I bumped into the wall and turning left. We found our way up but even at the last corner my wheel and one foot were in the bog before I realised that we'd reached the corner. Half way down from the corner we saw the ghostly emanation from the hurricane lamp Daisy had put in the window. It was a quarter to four and we had left Llanrhystyd before half past ten!

I was wet from the knees down and round the neck but the raincoat had stood up marvellously. The walk had worn off the effects of beer and when Daisy had given me the coffee she had ready we went to bed. She had been worried, very naturally, and her mother had fussed a bit. Not a very good performance when one's mother-in-law is visiting.

Met Ifan at Bryncewyll after tea.

Wednesday 8th August

Walked to Bronant pleasantly in the morning for rations. Worked on Welsh versification in the evening. The appendix is a longer job than I thought but has finally cleared my mind on the differences between *rhupunt* and *cyhydedd hir* and that sort of thing.

Thursday 9th August

Rained. Did some more work and in the evening roasted duck shot by Ifan yesterday. Yesterday afternoon we made a haystack (Ifan, Dai Morus and I) in Cae Matthew and Dai made it narrow and, threatened by rain, of a phenomenal height. We wonder whether it will stand. So far it decorates the north-eastern skyline like a Dutch house. When it settles we'll thatch it.

Friday 10th August

Worked on Welsh verse all morning. After lunch Daisy and I set off for Llanddeiniol via Blaennant, Felincwm and Grip. Felincwm is obviously very old and a delightful spot in a steep wooded valley with a little meadow. Although lost to the world it's a grocer's shop and Auntie Mary tonight told us the romantic story of the woman who keeps it. Her lover went away years ago, married, separated from his wife and then returned. He is now getting old but they associate openly and she looks after his house, for he lives near.

We left the Wyre following a path up a steep hillside to Grip. Down in the next valley we bathed our feet in a pretty ford surrounded by trees with a piece of open green on either side.

Llanddeiniol is an exceptionally well-built village, perhaps as a result of the Carrog slate. The vicarage is one of the loveliest houses I've seen with lovely windows and delicately used stone. If I wanted to live in a village I'd try to get a house there. Daisy made a pretty collection of wild flowers and we caught a bus at Cornel Ofan which took us to Lôn Sais.

Saturday 11th August

Worked on Welsh verse in the morning and sat over the fire at Pant Amlwg with Dai Morus all afternoon. Mist and drizzle. After tea went with Daisy for a shot at pigeons at Blaenwyre but not one came near. Ifan caught a trout in the Camddwr and David set a nightline on Llyn Eiddwen.

Sunday 12th August

David took in his nightline before breakfast and came back with six good eels, one monster, and a trout. So fried eels for breakfast. Prepared broth and made three pounds of gooseberry and rhubarb jam which was treacly owing to the dark brown sugar and generally scoffed at. They shall have their shop jam tomorrow.

Finished the verse appendix by three and plan to post it to Fabers tomorrow. Now I can write something else. Went up to Hafod Ithel before tea, a fine windy afternoon. David has really got down to the boat today and there's some prospect of seeing it afloat before the summer ends.

Daisy made excellent curried eels for supper.

Monday 13th August

Ifan went off with Dai Morus early, invited to shoot grouse in Llyfnant valley. I went out thinking that duck might be driven up from Glanteify but only got a snipe on Blaencamddwr pool.

Town midday and Daisy had a tooth out under gas and happy about it. Saw Megan and Maldwyn and made arrangements for Snowdon. They brought us home.

Tuesday 14th August

Ifan and Dai Morus didn't get a shot yesterday. I started my short story on the burning of England. Daisy baked two beautiful cakes and I a rabbit and bacon pie with pastry by Daisy and delicious. Ifan made a vain journey to Mynydd Brith for grouse.

Wednesday 16th August

Last night the moon came up a slice of lemon; tonight it's a candied orange.

Daisy and I had a good day today. We set out at eight by bus to Aber, caught the ten o'clock to Cwm Ystwyth via Devil's Bridge and walked down the

31

Ystwyth valley. We took the lower Hafod drive and almost immediately met a dozen ponies on our path, wild, free things of several colours, with a very feminine long-haired white one in the lead. We watched logs being dragged down the opposite hillside. The denuding proceeds and soon the forestry commission will have lined it up and down with conifers as neat as a backroom blueprint. There are still splendid beeches and oaks and large groups of birches, which I've only met before in such profusion in the poetry of Dafydd ap Gwilym. We turned in to see the ruins of the old mansion. Much still stands for only the lead from the roof, the glass and the floor planks have been removed but a few winters will see to the rest. The clock tower had been blown up for some reason and lay sprawled across the terrace into the park, columns of green porphyry and masses of brickwork mixed with carved freestone. Sheep lay in the long central room away from sun and flies and when we looked down a corridor to a verandah there was a huge dark billy goat looking in at us. His horns were really antlers, two feet long, flat, rising clear of his head and curving out in perfect proportion. He had a great black beard and Robinson Crusoe trousers. Having had a good look at us he moved slowly off, stopping to scratch his back with a horn or to nip off a thistle head. Daisy followed at a respectful distance to try to sketch him. We were told at the pub at Pontrhydygroes later that he roams the park and that she-goats are brought to him. He is dangerous, the man said. Six jays flew squawking over our heads as we left Hafod House for the Bont.

Friday 17th August

In the afternoon Daisy and I did a quiet mushroom hunt and Ifan took out the gun. In the evening Daisy baked and Dai Morus and I set out for Garn Wen. Just beyond Pwll yr Ych we spotted an unshorn sheep badly fly-blown, one of Rhydfudr's, and Dai went back for shears. I went on but didn't get a shot though I waited an hour near the little lake. I heard two shots from Blaencamddwr direction and guessed that Dai had gone there since it was too late to follow me. He got two duck but only found one in the darkness without a dog. A red moon came up and bog and mountain glowed strangely as I walked home. Juby was very lively and snuffled thoroughly around the shores of the pool.

Today I finished a story about the burning of England and the return of the cattle along the drovers' roads.

Sunday 19th August

Cemented around the sink and fixed in the pipe. In the afternoon walked over to Cae Mathew and watched a family of little owls.

Monday 20th August

Snowdon excursion. 8.15 Bus to Aber. Megan and Maldwyn ready to leave 9.30. Arrived Llanberis 12.30. Excellent lunch at the Castle Hotel, a house decorated in very good taste and with good pictures carefully lit. Chicken soup, cold salmon and salad, potatoes, cabbage and swede, fruit jelly and cream, black coffee, with a bottle of Bass — my lunch.

Queued at 2 for the little train and moved slowly on till 3.45 when we got on. Would have much preferred to walk up the mountain but the train journey was exciting enough an experience. Excellent visibility to within ¼ mile of the summit and then thick cloud. We could see all Anglesey and Lleyn running down to its point in the sea.

At the top in the bleak mist-drenched hotel were hundreds of people either queuing for the return trip or for tea. Very few people outside where a bitterly cold wind was blowing and the mist accentuated the cages of the little platform and cairn. Just before we left the mist on the return journey I saw a golden eagle swerve towards us and away. When we got out into sunshine we took photographs.

We got down to Llanberis by seven and left soon after. Back through Capel Curig and Betws y Coed. Stopped at Blaenau Ffestiniog for chips and got back to Aber by 10.45. Maldwyn brought us home.

Tuesday 21st August

A quiet day, our heads more weary than our bodies, since we didn't walk enough. Ifan and Dai Morus sheep dipping at Bancllyn.

Wednesday 22nd August

Went on with the hedge trimming. Uncle Dan told me two stories in the potato field.

1. Guto Carreg yr Ast, a South Walian, was the best runner in Wales. One day he ran a race against two horses, with heavy bets against him. He won and his sweetheart ran to congratulate him and clapped him on the back. The winded Guto dropped dead.

2. The better known story of Dick Penderyn. Dick had a rival for a girl and one night during the Chartist troubles in Glamorgan was out when a policeman was killed. Dick's knife was found in the policeman's side and Dick was tried and hanged at Cardiff, the last public execution in Wales. He was buried at St Mary's Aberavon. Years afterwards a Welsh minister in America was called to a dying man's bedside. He confessed to the murder of the policeman. The preacher returned to Wales, cleared Dick Penderyn's name, and preached a sermon from his grave in Aberavon.

Daisy and I went over to Llwynrhyddod after lunch to cut a linepost. As we got back a car came up and Jack Lloyd Jones and his family hailed us. We had a cheerful tea together and then all went up Hafod Ithel. Took Jack and his son John down to Tangraig, where they were all amazed that a headmaster could be so unassuming.

Thursday 23rd August

Postcards from Christopher Sandford in France and Mam in Nottinghamshire. Went shopping to Aber and back soon. Posted the appendix on Welsh prosody to Fabers. Bought wine for my birthday tomorrow.

Ifan and Dai Morus set off on bikes at 7.30 for the Nantrhwch sheep dog trials. When we got back at 5.30 my bike, which Dai was using, was in the hedge. There had been no lorry up from Tregaron as they had hoped and Dai Morus had come disconsolately back. Ifan went on by bike and got back at 10.30.

Friday 24th August

Thick cloud and a driving wind. Waited at Bryn Amlwg for the meat van. Morning at home, Daisy sewing and Ifan arranging his [fishing] flies. Daisy gave me a very good hairbrush for my birthday and Mam and Megan sent cards. A splendid supper — jugged hare, pancakes and marzipan cake with a good Graves and Australian burgundy. Dai Morus helped us with it.

Saturday 25th August

Baked in the morning, beef for cold eating, cakes and pies. Strong south wind and heavy rain, the roughest August I remember. Stayed in in the afternoon. After tea to Tangraig where Uncle Dan told us how his grandmother used to walk to London to weed gardens. A bath of warm rainwater (Daisy in it now) before going to bed.

Sunday 26th August

Spent mostly in talk and listening to Dai Morus' account of his trip to Cardiff in the van with Davies Gorslwyd.

Monday 27th August

Down to Aber to meet Daisy's friends the Holmeses. Big shopping and Daisy had two teeth filled.

Tuesday 28th August

Awake early after a disturbed night to a broadside of toys hurled from the bed above. Michael, aged 1½ learnt immediately how to work the bellows and was quiet for a long time in the morning puffing as long as I held the lower handle for him. In the afternoon Charlie and I went up to Blaenwyre to help Dai Morus separate sheep. I got some more mushrooms to add to the good bag of the morning.

Wednesday 29th August

Set off at about 10.30 for St David's and got to White

Sands Bay before two having stopped for a drink at Fishguard. Saw several standing stones on the way. Daisy and I walked to the edge of St David's Head and on the way back found graves, ancient walls and stone alignments. Looking down one of the cliffs we saw a very fine razorbill waddling along and flapping his wings. A little one had been washed ashore at White Sands Bay and was being mobbed by gulls. It couldn't fly so we chased the gulls away and the little razorbill paddled off out to sea again, leaning forward and using its stumpy wings as oars. The sheep were all severely hobbled, perhaps to save them from being panicked over the cliffs by town-dwelling dogs on holiday.

We spent a good deal of time in the Cathedral and I was pleased to find the tombs and effigies of men I had been reading about for my book, the Lord Rhys, Edmund Tudor, Gruffudd Gryg, Gerald the Welshman. An excellent blend of solidity and delicacy and more restful to the eye than most cathedrals. Had no time to go around the lovely Bishop's Palace but bought a new guide to South Wales monuments at the door.

Stopped in Cardigan on the way back and over a pint of beer at the Saddlers exchanged reminiscences of George Rees, Joe Cryer and Jim Williams with the company. Stopped again at the Red Lion at Llanrhystyd and were home by nine, the children behaving pretty well.

Thursday 30th August

A day at home. Dai Morus, Tommy Oliver and Uncle Dan spent the day making a new gutter under the road half way down the road. Swam in the lake before lunch with Barbara, Charlie and the children.

Friday 31st August

Showed our visitors the way back to Ponterwyd avoiding Aberystwyth, via Lledrod, Llanilar, Cwm Newidion and Devil's Bridge. Abandoned our plans of exploring the old fort owing to sheets of rain and took a bus to Aberystwyth. In the bus a rather continental looking chap asked me whether I knew French. When I said I did he said, " I thought you might." He wanted me to translate a letter from a French woman congratulating him on his new book and asking permission to use passages in France. The book was about the Afghan wolf hound and was full of pictures of elegant persons with these huge dogs, Madge Titheradge one of them. The author, Clifford Hubbard, lives at Ponterwyd, is re-learning Welsh, which he spoke as a child, and has written a book on the Cardiganshire corgi which is also appearing in Welsh.

Back at Aberystwyth we met George Green and Dan Fronfynwent. I bought *Baledi Morganwg* [Glamorgan Ballads].

Saturday 1st September

Dai Morus doesn't like it that the first has passed with not a shot fired but we don't know of any partridge near here.

Spent the afternoon carrying posts with Dai Morus to be sawn up at Tynewydd and then reeds for the haystack up at Cae Mathew. The house is peaceful, especially without the patter of little bums falling wallop off the bed above our heads. Yet I found the children, especially alone, more tolerable than their parents. Most children are more sensible than their parents or at least have more compensatory charm for their stupidities.

Sunday 2nd September

Wrote letters, Terence Tiller, Alan Pringle, National Insurance, Cooks. Sketched with Daisy in the afternoon. In the evening with Daisy and Dai to Blaenwyre where we had a marvellous view with the telescope of

the mountains to the north and east. Then at Pant yr Ala we collected several pounds of mushrooms. Ate a large quantity for supper.

Talked with Mam and Ifan over the phone after supper. Mam very well and cheerful after her trip to Wheatley and Port Talbot. A pleasant walk back to the house and an evening of promising calm.

Dai Morus had artificial insemination for his Welsh black heifer this morning. Daisy wonders if this isn't Sabbath-breaking with sex rampant. Dai usually takes his cows to a bull (cost 5/- instead of 25/-) but he wanted a Welsh Black and Saunders' Welsh Black bull is still too young. The others nearby are all Shorthorns. When the vet came he had run out of Welsh Black semen and brought Hereford. I wonder how many generations of cows will accept the vet for the bull, until the Pasiphae situation has to be reversed.

Monday 3rd September

To Aberystwyth by the one o'clock bus, Auntie Mary with us. Whilst we waited for the bus she told me about her two years' service in London when she was eighteen and nineteen.

Daisy shopped, etc. and I copied a poem from Thomas Prys' manuscript to translate for the BBC. Greatly amused by Prys' poem on his unfortunate sea battle.

Tuesday 4th September

Another afternoon on Thomas Prys and Wm Middleton's Psalms, Daisy with me reading archaeology. Near the Post Office we met Clifford Hubbard, the dog writer, who said he was packing up to go to Australia. I asked whether it was in pursuit of dingoes and he said that he had kept one at Ponterwyd that had killed a lot of sheep and that he was selling furniture to pay for them before he left.

Dai Morus went to Lampeter and after a few pints went to the Agricultural Offices to claim the four pounds odd they owe him. He started by letting them know what he thought of them and the whole system of controls but got little satisfaction out of them.

Wednesday 5th September

Dai got a letter saying that Lampeter credited him with the money against future work supplied by them. This is to cover up their error and he's furious, talking of a lawyer's letter. He went off to Bancllyn in great style this morning in the trap with two lambs to be castrated.

I translated the Thomas Prys poem yesterday and corrected it and made a fair copy today.

This evening Daisy and I went with Dai in the *gambo* to get his posts from Tynewydd and talked to Mam and Ifan on the phone. He's going to get us seats for the ballet when we go to London.

Talked to Dick Porthmawr, who had come looking for Dai Morus this morning. He asked why I thought all these English people were buying places in West Wales. I told him of the remark I'd heard that English names don't appear much on tombstones, i.e. they don't stay long; and he said "Yes, they're like elephants. They go off somewhere to die."

We're all very pleased at the demonstration against the War Office at Trawsfynydd the other day.

Thursday 6th September

Daisy and I went up to the Library at 11.30 taking sandwiches and tea. I stayed on till five copying more Thomas Prys and chasing references to tobacco smoking.

(The death of Daniel Hopkin reported. A London magistrate latterly (born Llantwit Major) and wreaths were sent to his funeral by the prostitutes who had been humanly treated by him. The Oxford Street barrow boys sent a floral chair surmounted by a golden crown. Did ever a judge have such tributes?)

From Aberystwyth Daisy went to the Talybont factory for wool and thence home. I took a bus to Tregaron where Dai Morus had gone to the sheep dog trials. The sheep were wild and stubborn in the evening and even the best dog handlers (Daniels, Ystradgynlais, for instance, with the dog which won the supreme championship of Britain) could do little with them.

Went down to the Railway Tavern with Dai Morus and Ianto Llocau and drank beer in good company until bus time. Made the best of our way home over the mountain from Bronant, the night fine but the rough ground difficult. Daisy had soupe à l'oignon gratinée ready for us when we got in soon after ten.

Friday 7th September

A quiet day at home. Daisy did a wash and I went to Blaenwyre with Dai and got some good mushrooms at Pant yr Ala.

Saturday 8th September [Daisy's birthday]

In the morning loaded the wool with Dai Morus (about sixty pounds' worth) and Daisy and I went with him and it to Bancllyn over the mountain. The castrator was there and the young bull was fetched in from the field looking very wild. There is some mixture of breed in him, a touch of Hereford with the basic Shorthorn, and he wouldn't pass the ministry test for a certificate, though he has been doing his work very well.

In the afternoon went in to Aberystwyth and after tea to the opera, *Faust*, done by the Welsh National Opera Company at the King's Hall. Excellent singing and acting, and the parts unusually well cast, but pathetically mean and conventional décor and costumes. The Arts Council should make improvement here a condition of their support. We made pleasant excursions to the White Horse and Blue Bell for refreshment and finished up at the Railway Tavern whilst waiting for Morris Llain to take his girl back to Llanbadarn. We bought chips and were carried home in great style after an excellent evening.

Sunday 9th September

Blaenwyre in the afternoon. Dai Morus in the house a good deal so much reminiscence and mountain politics.

Monday 10th September

Walked over to Bronant after lunch to catch the bus to Lampeter. Got across before the rain and waited at the Paddington shop. A quiet evening at Gorlan. I walked to Cwmann for a pint of beer before supper.

Tuesday 11th September

Daisy and I took a bus to Cellan in the morning and walked back looking for mushrooms. Saw none so picked a few pounds of blackberries, the first of the season.

In the afternoon I typed the Thomas Prys poem and translation for the BBC. After supper walked to Troed y Rhiw to meet Jack Lloyd Jones for a few pints. Listened afterwards to the first performance of Stravinsky's *Rake's Progress* from Venice, the family having gone to bed. Daisy bought a hat and a grey pullover in the afternoon.

Wednesday 12th September

Out shopping in the morning and took Daisy to see my father's grave. The granite looks well amongst the new-fashioned shiny black horrors.

After lunch took the bus to Aberystwyth and had tea with the Tom Joneses. Back home by the five o'clock bus. Heard that David had arrived and was sitting an exam.

Thursday 13th September

David came in after breakfast having slept with Dai Morus, not wanting to disturb us. I opened ditches around the house and dug a new hole in the bower. After lunch Uncle Dan called and asked if we wanted to walk over the mountain to Blaenavon with him to shop. In spite of a howling south wind we went and had to push our way hard against it until we got off the mountain. Whilst we were in the shop it began to rain and we came back along the road in stinging but not heavy rain. The whole way Uncle Dan pointed out derelict houses and told us who lived there when he was a boy and there were a hundred children at Tangarreg School, Blaenpennal.

Yesterday we saw a strange character. As the bus came into the main road at Temple Bar we met a man on a bicycle. He was tall and sallow, with a furtive look in his eye. Where there were holes in his suit his skin showed and on his head he wore a sort of skull cap of sacking with bits hanging down over his ears. He carried a huge sack behind his saddle and a smaller one before him. He heard people in the bus discussing him, for he is well known. He sometimes puts down a sort of sackcloth veil over his eyes to avoid seeing women. In the sack there is a portable wireless set. When we told Dai Morus about him, he remembered having passed him at Rhydrhoser two years ago and having had trouble with his pony because of the man's strange appearance and the noise of his radio. Dai wonders why he doesn't go to live in some cabin in the hills. It must be very troublesome for him, he says, to avoid seeing women on the main road. One day he'll run into a bus through keeping his eyes down, Dai said. And I added, And then wake up to find a nurse washing him.

September 14th (wedding anniversary) — 24th summarized

Ifan and his friend Dennis arrived on Friday 14th. We postponed our bonfire celebration because of the rain.

On Saturday we started the bonfire but it never got really going since things were still wet and the thorns weren't dead. But it did cook us potatoes and amuse Dai Morus on his way back from Pontrhydfendigaid sheep dog trials.

Not having been round behind the island once this summer I went round three times in 24 hours. Ifan had heard duck coming in at dusk whilst preparing to go home after fishing and Dai and he and I went up to wait for them. I've never seen the water so high around the lake and I was silly enough to cross the bog to the Brynhebrysg side and lucky enough to get out of it in the darkness. Dai fired at and dropped a duck which we never found, Ifan in pitch darkness killed an overhead mallard drake and waded up to his waist to get it out of the rushes. I didn't get a shot. I went up alone in the morning and again in the evening with Dai and I only fired at some awkward snipe and missed three or four. Dai got nothing.

David and Ifan got a large number of rabbits, over twenty, and one hare, which we ate when the Sandfords came. David sold his rabbits for pocket money. We gave the Tom Joneses lunch at the Black Lion on Tuesday 18th very successfully and I did a long session at the Library on Arthurian stuff.

On Wednesday Christopher Sandford brought his son and daughter and two dogs from Leominster to lunch and tea, and the day passed happily. They have made a legend of our life on the mountain.

I spent pleasant and unhurried hours with Dai Morus at the oats, carrying what had been cut ten days before and cutting more with the scythe, with Dai binding behind me. Much separating and judging of sheep and lambs too and the introduction of a new ram who got a good drubbing from the old ones.

During the last week (17th — 24th) the greenfinches sang beautifully all round the house. The heather is nearly over but there are still whinberries. Daisy and I had a very successful cranberry picking afternoon on Banc Tynant, since the Llyn people have stripped our usual patch in Pant Arthur.

Daisy's new glasses (birthday present) arrived, having once had to be sent back, and look very good, a new shape and a light bilberry stain in colour.

Terence has sent on the Thomas Prys material, introduction, text and translation, to the Third Programme committee.

Fabers sent criticisms of my book on Welsh poetry but are preparing an estimate and an offer. They suggest I see Prof. Idris Foster (Celtic, Oxford) who turns out to be their expert, for his recommendations on one or two points. He has strongly approved of the book.

Tuesday 25th September

To Lampeter with Daisy per Morris Llain.

Wednesday 26th September

Daisy leaves for Leamington. I type modifications to my book all day and have a good hour at Ram Inn with Jack Lloyd Jones.

Thursday 27th September

I go to London. Evening at the Metropolitan Music Hall. A good comedian — Jimmy Guy.

Friday 28th September

I do the Egyptian Education Office in the morning and

then a long session with Alan Pringle of Fabers. We agree upon most points. Bar and lunch with Terence at the Stag's Head.

Met Daisy at Paddington and after tea down to Sheen Lane to Bessie's to see Bet and Tessie. Sherry and supper there. Too late to go on to Reggie Smith's at St John's Wood.

Saturday 29th September

Collected passports and tickets etc. in the morning. In the afternoon to Sudbury to see the London Welsh beat the Wasps. A fine afternoon and a rare experience for us. In the evening to Covent Garden for the last night of the Saddlers Wells Ballet *Daphnus and Chloe*, a lively ballet with good décor by John Craxton. Most impressed by Alexander Grant's dancing. Shearer skinny and impassive. English ballerinas don't seem to feel.

Sunday 30th September

Petticoat Lane in the morning — a dreadful crowd. Ate stewed eels and bought Daisy a long string of ivory beads. I worked in the afternoon and she slept. Went out without having tea to go to a city church for Bach cantatas and Daisy fainted in the heat of the Paddington tube. She was very soon right so we had tea and abandoned the music.

Monday 1st October

I went to Oxford to meet Idris Foster who turned out to be very nice and helpful and most enthusiastic about my book which he will use for the projected course in Mediaeval Welsh which will be optional for the English Schools. Suggested a rewriting of the Arthurian section as an appendix and agreed with my stand against Fabers over footnotes.

Tuesday 2nd October

I worked at the recasting of my notes and finished them. In the evening to the Old Vic to see *Tamburlaine* (Tyrone Guthrie adaptation and production) which we greatly enjoyed. Wolfit beastly and powerful as Tamburlaine and a fine baroque décor by Harry.

Wednesday 3rd October

To Paris and a pleasant crossing. A good meal and early to bed.

Thursday 4th October

A lazy morning and the Louvre in the afternoon, concentrating on the Greek sculpture.

Friday 5th October

A compartment to ourselves so as good a night as can be expected. A good room at the Graspo de Ua. Dinner at the fish and delicatessen shop behind the Doge's Palace.

Saturday 6th October

In the morning to the Tiepolo exhibition. Most impressed by the eighteenth-century ensemble of the Rezzonico Palace with the Tiepolo ceilings and a remarkable picture (*Death of Darius*) by Tiepolo's contemporary Giovanni Battista Piazzetta.

In the afternoon by *piroscafo* to Torcello, of a charm out of this world. The green *campo* with children playing on the scraps of ancient stonework, the age of the buildings, the amazing twelfth-century mosaics of Doomsday and the Apostles and the Virgin, with the approach along the winding canal through fields made us decide to come again to sketch and soak in the atmosphere.

In the evening aboard the *Campidoglio* [to sail to Egypt].

Notes on People and Places

Mynydd Bach
On this moorland ridge between Cardigan Bay and the Cambrian Mountains, areas of common land survived the nineteenth-century enclosures — a fact recorded in folk memories of the "Sais Bach" who failed to seize land from the local people. It has lakes, rare birds, a neolithic burial site, as well as a rich recent cultural history that includes the poet E. Prosser Rhys, one of "Beirdd y Mynydd Bach" (The Mynydd Bach Poets). It is a special place even to those without local roots; to Gwyn Williams, with his Mynydd Bach ancestry and lifelong attachment, it was a spiritual home.

Daisy [Williams]
Although she had been born to English parents in New York and spent most of an itinerant childhood in England, Mynydd Bach became home for Daisy too

after she met Gwyn in Egypt. As an artist, most notably using textiles and indigo dye, she derived much of her inspiration from the mountain landscape and in particular the area around Llyn Eiddwen.

Auntie Mary [Jones]
Gwyn's father's cousin, Dai Morus's mother. She, her husband Uncle Dan and her daughter Bet lived at Tangraig and were the nearest neighbours to Blaenbeidog. She was, according to Gwyn, "the kindest woman I have ever known".

David [Williams]
Gwyn's elder son from his first marriage; he was a student of agriculture at University College of Wales, Aberystwyth at this time. Later he worked at the college and farmed on Mynydd Bach where he still lives in retirement. His sons and his grandchildren have continued the family attachment to the mountain.

Uncle Dan [Jones]
Auntie Mary's husband, Dai Morus's father. A stonemason who taught Gwyn how to build a dry-stone wall.

Ifan [Williams]
Gwyn's second son from his first marriage; a student of philosophy at University College of Wales, Aberystwyth at this time. He and his wife Dorothy also have strong links with Mynydd Bach.

Mari [Edwards] Waungron
A local character who lived alone, simply and in traditional fashion in Waungron, the house in Trefenter where Daisy's mother later lived for many years.

Dai Morus [Jones]
Gwyn's second cousin, son of Auntie Mary and Uncle Dan. Born and brought up on Mynydd Bach, he spent a short time as a miner in south Wales where he was unhappy and was reputed to have walked back to Trefenter. There he lived a life of trapping and farming, fishing and shooting until his death at the age of ninety-one. Like his sister Bet, who also lived to the age of ninety-one, he never married. From his home at Pantamlwg, and later Blaenbeidog, he travelled, often to game fairs but also as far as Istanbul once with Gwyn and his family, and he took a lively interest in politics and world affairs. Gwyn's lifelong friend (they were the same age), he was a playmate during summer holidays when they were children and a drinking and shooting companion in adulthood. One of their childhood pranks, which Gwyn remembered in his autobiography, was to chase a pig into Pantffynnon, Dai Morus's family home at that time, "to elicit loud *ychafis* from his grandmother". As the description of the drunken return from Llanrhystud in the *Summer Journal* shows, their complicity continued into middle age. Their arguments were amicable but often quite heated as Dai Morus's right-wing political views contrasted with Gwyn's.

Jack Lloyd Jones
Headmaster of Lampeter School and friend of Gwyn.

Megan and Maldwyn [Hughes]
Gwyn's youngest sister and brother-in-law. Their long working and married life was spent in Lampeter, where Gwyn and Daisy often stayed with them en route by train to south Wales and beyond. They frequently visited Mynydd Bach with their sons Alun and

Rhys, on early closing day when they could leave their shop, Rhys Hughes & Son. Megan now lives at Clarach, near Aberystwyth.

Gwyn Jones
Professor of English at Aberystwyth at this time. He and his first wife, Alice, were occasional, rather glamorous, visitors to Gwyn's home on Mynydd Bach.

Tom Jones
Professor of Welsh at Aberystwyth.

Morris [Jones] Llain
Lived and farmed at Llain in Trefenter and ran an essential taxi service between Trefenter and Aberystwyth, and later to the villages and towns spread over mid Wales where Gwyn taught extra-mural classes from 1952-5.

Enid and Tommy [Davies]
Gwyn's second sister and brother-in-law. Tommy was headmaster of Pontgarreg School.

Ieuan Williams
Gwyn's brother, vicar of North Wheatley, Nottingham-shire, at this time. Ieuan now lives near Oxford.

Dilys and Stan [Rees]
Gwyn's eldest sister and brother-in-law. Stan was an engineer in the steel works at Port Talbot. Dilys had trained and worked as a teacher before her marriage, after which she continued to be involved in the cultur-al life of the town and the chapel.

Tommy Oliver
A builder who lived and kept a smallholding at Brynamlwg.

Terence Tiller
Writer, friend of Gwyn from Cairo. He was a member of the Cairo team in the verse war in which Gwyn and friends in Alexandria and Cairo engaged during the winter of 1943-4 (see *Flyting in Egypt: The Story of a Verse War 1943-44*, Gwyn Williams, Alun Books, 1991).

Alan Pringle
Gwyn's editor at Faber and Faber for many years.

Christopher Sandford
Owner of the Golden Cockerell Press which published Gwyn's *In Defence of Women* and *Against Women*. He and his wife Lettice were friends of Gwyn who lived at Eye Manor, near Leominster. Their son Jeremy later wrote for TV and radio, including the play *Cathy Come Home*.

Bessie, Bet and Tessie
Bessie was Gwyn's father's cousin who lived in London. Bet, daughter of Uncle Dan and Auntie Mary, lived at Tangraig; Tessie (Teresa Livermore) joined the family at Tangraig as an evacuee during the Second World War and stayed on.

CARDIGAN
BAY

BORTH

ABERYSTWYTH

DEVIL'S BRIDGE

LLANILAR

LLANGWYRYFON

LLEDROD

LLANRHYSTUD

Wyre

M Y N Y D D   B A C H

TREFENTER

LLYN
EIDDWEN

BRONNANT

ABERAERON

TREGARON

4 MILES

4 KILOMETRES

LAMPETER

58

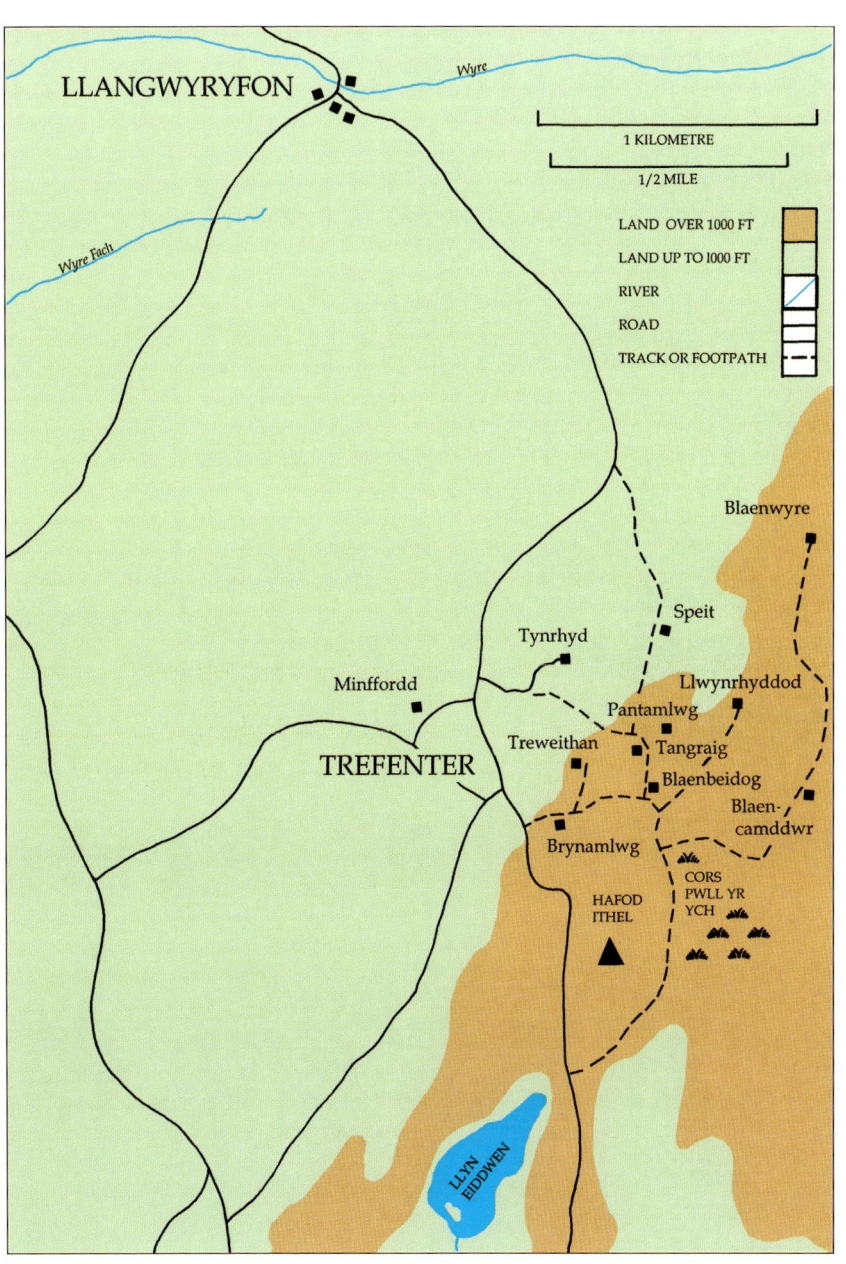

LLANGWYRYFON

Wyre

Wyre Fach

1 KILOMETRE

1/2 MILE

LAND OVER 1000 FT
LAND UP TO 1000 FT
RIVER
ROAD
TRACK OR FOOTPATH

Blaenwyre

Speit

Tynrhyd

Minffordd

Llwynrhyddod

Pantamlwg

TREFENTER

Treweithan

Tangraig

Blaenbeidog

Blaen-
camddwr

Brynamlwg

CORS
PWLL YR
YCH

HAFOD
ITHEL

LLYN
EIDDWEN

Afterword

The summer of 1951 was the last which Gwyn and Daisy were to spend on Mynydd Bach free of the cares and concerns of work and family life. In 1952 Trefenter unexpectedly became their permanent home when political events in Egypt in January of that year led to a forced "exodus" when they left Alexandria "not wishing much ever to see it again" (19 January, "Exodus 1952").

The winters were much harder than the idyllic summers, as Gwyn's later diaries show. Gwyn and Daisy returned to Wales in February 1952, with their first child expected within two months, snow on the ground and heating urgently needed. Llwynrhyddod was a soundly built house but had no electricity or running water and was a mile across fields and along stone tracks from the nearest tarmac road. Peat, coal and wood were the only fuels for heating and cooking.

Peat Gwyn cut and dried on the mountain and carried home in a sack on his back. Coal and wood were delivered to the end of the track two fields away at Blaenbeidog (where they had stayed during previous summers) and then carried by the bucketload until someone with a tractor could be persuaded to cart it the last few hundred yards. In November 1954 there is "No hope of getting coal across yet, so I go over in blinding rain with two buckets." (27.11.54) One day in January the postman "gets through but yesterday he fell into a drift and was seen cursing and drying his frozen clothes at Minffordd in the afternoon". (28.1.54) Even in summer there could be echoes of Caradoc Evans's stories: Gwyn records the story of Anne y Bryn, whose body had been found in a field after she died of heart failure: "They carried her body into the house that night and since there were no relatives she was left alone. The rats got at her face and so she was laid out in the chapel to await her funeral." (8.7.54)

In spring, summer and autumn, though, there were days on the mountain and in the garden with the children interspersed with days working at the National Library. The complete entry for 4 June 1954 consists of: "Typing, peat and garden." On July 9 he records: "At odd moments I'm now assembling, completing and revising full length translations mostly of *cywyddau* to offer to Fabers." This is followed, on 10 July, by a day in the garden:

I transplant clarkia, marigolds and nasturtiums. Huge cos lettuce from the garden and good radish. Soon peas and beans.

A heron settles in the rhos and we get a good view of it preening through the telescope.

Gardening, shooting and fishing, which had been leisure pursuits during summer holidays on Mynydd Bach, now became essential to self-sufficiency on a small income. Unusually for a father in the 1950s, Gwyn was able to spend whole days and weeks with his children, becoming involved in their lives as they were in his. The whole family walked, gardened and tobogganed together without the restrictions of a nine-to-five job.

It was during these years on the mountain that Gwyn published his *Introduction to Welsh Poetry*. He also worked on his own poems and further translation, and on plays and talks, mainly for radio. As well as providing some income, radio was an important link with the wider world. Gwyn records listening to rugby matches while gardening, to innovative drama, such as *Under Milk Wood* which gave him hope that his own work might be appreciated, and to music. Following the broadcast of a concert from the Festival Hall, he comments: "Marvellous to have it at one's own hearth with a glass of one's own beer at hand." There were frequent trips away, too, often to record radio programmes, to Swansea, Cardiff, London and Oxford. Gwyn usually went alone, leaving Daisy at home, sometimes with relatives or friends, to look after the children. But he compensated for her evident longing for some contact with a more sophisticated life by recording for her in letters and in his diary the details of the clothes worn by women he met in academic and publishing circles. Even Aberystwyth could provide a glimpse of the latest fashion: "Discussion of M.A. work in the morning. Alice for lunch — black crepe wool frock — bright red bolero — Audrey Hepburn fringe — shiny black straw muffin hat and short veil!" (10.4.55)

Gwyn's diaries of 1954 and 1955 show the increasing

worries of life on the mountain, with its practical diffi-culties of living on income from writing and part-time further education lecturing and of surviving harsh winters in what even then were seen as primitive con-ditions. Gwyn's concern with the common illnesses of himself and the family and with staying indoors when unwell is perhaps related to his paternal grandfather's death on Mynydd Bach at an early age following a "chill" caught when out in the rain. References to the weather, heating and fuel are a constant in the diaries. In January 1955:

The wood I ordered came yesterday as far as Blaenbeidog. Now the usual trouble over the final quarter of a mile. Jack Tynrhyd promises to come after dinner. He does but fails to get up the hill past Bryn Gwartheg where there's a glacier, now the snow has blown off for thirty or forty yards. I carry three loads of wood on my back in a blizzard and we have a pine wood fire. Will this convince me that we can't spend another winter here? (5.1.55)

But he was still making improvements to their basic living conditions; on 9 January, "I work on the tŷ bach with good pieces of wood and start on the door. It's very cold and I'm driven in about three o'clock with frozen feet, but the frame of the door is done." And there are compensations, even in winter; on 14 January

Followed a badger back for 100 yards past the house in the snow. I spend the whole day out. All morning around Llyn Eiddwen, where I see 29 geese (Canada?), 12 mallard, 6 teal and 2 coot without getting within range of anything. A beau-tiful sunny blue morning with a dusting of snow over every-thing and the edges of the lake frozen, up to 50 yards at each end.

Even people who had lived in Trefenter all their lives, though, thought that Llwynrhyddod, several hundred feet higher and wilder than the village, was uninhabitable; Jac y Pentre and his father helped carry coal to the house:

His father thinks this a hell of a place to live in. When I said one disadvantage of living here was not having a spare room for visitors he said "Pwy uffern ddele yma i aros?" ["Who the hell would come here to stay?"] (20.9.54)

On New Year's Eve 1953 Gwyn appreciates the "disregarding calm at five past twelve":

At midnight Daisy and I went out thinking we might hear some sound announcing the New Year, the cracked bell at Llangwyryfon, a railway engine whistling from Llanfarian or even Aberystwyth. It was a still clear night and the grass was crisp with frost under our feet. The stars were like splinters of cut glass and the moon was well out of sight behind Blaenwyre. There was no sound at all but the rustle of the brook down through the Speit cwm, sounding like a still sea breaking on shingle or a breeze through drying leaves. There was no light to be seen but Enlli winking across the water. Not many places in this island can have had such disregarding calm at five past twelve. The radio was playing "Hen Wlad fy Nhadau" and we got in just in time to turn off "God Save the Queen". We wished her no harm but she was not our concern at this moment.

A year later, however, the mood has changed. There is "Myxomatosis all round us" and walking to Llangwyryfon to shop he passes "a dozen dead rabbits", although there is still the excitement of seeing "the male hen-harrier four times in three days, a very beautiful bird, in colouring and flight". This New Year's Eve is gloomier: "Stayed up till twelve but Welsh radio dull. The preacher at midnight a fitting culmination to the wettest year yet." (31.12.54)

Throughout the autumn of 1954 and the early months of 1955 it is clear that Gwyn and Daisy were struggling with the question: "Shall we continue to live this way?" (1.1.55) Notices of jobs abroad arrive and on 29 January a "Lectureship at Makerere is the most attractive but I haven't quite got round to facing it yet." Only two weeks later, though, "I've now decided not to go abroad if I can possibly help it but to make the best of it in Aberystwyth with extra-mural work etc." (11.2.55) Eventually, in May 1955, by now with two children, the family moved to a flat in Borth and in January 1956 Gwyn took up the post of Professor of English at the University of Benghazi. Mynydd Bach remained the family's base, though, as they returned each summer from Libya and, later, Turkey to Llwynrhyddod until they bought Treweithan, which became a year-round home when Gwyn retired in 1969.

Gwyn continued to keep a diary for the rest of his life. Those from 1956 until his retirement, however, are skimpy and intermittent. In Libya he travelled, imbibed the archaeology of the area and threw himself into the life of the university; there cannot have been time. But he did write continuously and energetically in several genres. His volumes of translations from Welsh poetry (*The Burning Tree*, 1956; *Presenting Welsh Poetry*, 1959) were followed by novels and travel books also published by Faber. Moving to Istanbul again as Professor of English in 1961, he continued to write: criticism, novels, plays, a screenplay. His fullest diaries are on journeys, and he worked this material into three travel books on Turkey.

The freedom of retirement and coming back to Wales at a politically electric time gave him a new burst of energy; the diary habit too returned (and he wrote up to a page of A5 every day until within a year of his death over twenty years later). He lectured, gave poetry readings, presented television, and explored the

Celtic fringes. He began to see himself more as a poet, and wrote an autobiography in gazetteer form based on his life's wandering (*The ABC of (D.)G.W.*, Gomer, 1981). What he relished most though was the rediscovery, at last, of his roots. The section on Trefenter in his autobiography illustrates the sense of rootedness in family history which Mynydd Bach represented for Gwyn. When he traced the male line on his father's side, he found that "as far back as their occupation is mentioned they have been stone masons and builders". After buying Treweithan he was proud to discover that his grandfather and great-grandfather had built the house. In this piece he remembers childhood holidays as "the most exciting event in [the] family calendar".

Mynydd Bach and Llyn Eiddwen were "a playground" and many of the houses, with their "welcoming scent of peat fires" belonged to relatives or childhood friends of his father. So, when as an adult he came to choose his own home base, "Trefenter it had to be and was from the start". In 1930, on summer leave from Egypt, he had rented his first house in the village, Pentre Uchaf. Half a century later, when writing his autobiography, he described a lifetime's connection to the place and the family associations, still extending as the family grew with children, grandchildren and great-grand-children. Now living permanently in Trefenter he researched family history and local history. Within a year of moving back to Trefenter, he was writing his diary in Welsh.

Every day is a cocktail of cultural comment, family comings and goings along with observations on wildlife and the seasons. Noticing "yr haul yn machlud ddim ymhell o Enlli heno" ["the sun setting not far from Bardsey tonight", 17.6.74], he goes on to speculate whether the sun might reach the island for the summer solstice. But often the jubilance of this period of return, the *joie de vivre* to be found in his published work of this time, is undermined by more banal but pressing affairs in the diaries. Without mains water, with a private sup-ply that echoed both Heath Robinson and Jean de Florette, and what seems to have been a succession of long dry summers, the longing for rain was a constant drain on the Mynydd Bach dream. "Bennodd y dŵr yfed heddi. Er bod gwlith, niwl a glaw mân wedi cad-w'r tir yn wlyb, does dim glaw cyson wedi bod ers wythnosau." ["The drinking water came to an end today. Although dew, mist and drizzle have kept the ground damp, there's been no steady rain for weeks." 19.6.81]

The Gwyn Williams of the earlier Mynydd Bach diaries was in his late forties and early fifties, enjoying raising a second young family and revelling in the simple life of hunting and gathering, peat-cutting and the pounds of marmalade and the wine which Daisy seemed to make with such ease and with no electricity or running water. After 1969, he is growing old. His diaries have become in part a confidant for the tensions of married life, and later increasingly a record of his own physical decline. In 1983 Gwyn and Daisy moved from Mynydd Bach into Aberystwyth, a decision made initially after the heavy snows of winter 1981-2. Following this the diary entries are still a full and impressive record, but there is a retreat from the broad horizon of the mountain to the author's urban study and eventually the workings of his ailing body, until, only three months before his death, he records a time when "Roeddwn i wedi dechre meddwl am y ffyrdd gallwn farw." ["I had started to think of the ways in which I could die." 2.9.90]

Gwyn Williams died in December 1990. Daisy continued to draw and paint the Welsh landscape, but her inspiration in the 1990s was more in the woodlands around Plas Tanybwlch, Maentwrog, and in the architectural details of Aberystwyth, than on Mynydd Bach. She found her art now in the company of friends, without the companionship of Gwyn on the mountain. She died in 2001.

TW & LG

ASPECTS OF NOW
(A poem for the telephone)

The moment is now
you can test it all by now
by how things are now.

There can't be any other moment
though how would seem to be surrounded
by future, contemporary and past,
the parts of a verb, a way of saying.

No, it's all here now, so judge it
now you have it, now. I am part of it
for you and you for me since
you are listening. Listen to now.

Now for this world faltering
from growth to fission, for Wales too
in its greenness and intimacy, from
the bowelled smoke of the south to

the sliced stone of the north. Now
with some valleys drowned and some still human,
with a drover still living and buses
that cross the sea, with more trees

than sheep, with a language still alive now
which to our shame I'm not using now.
This is the moment to hold these things
in balance, to decide now which way

to allow or leash instinct, to tip
what we have into the scales now
knowing that now is the golden age
the only moment worth having. The now

if you like when I've stopped talking and
you're alone with now or with your lover
or friends or sheep or family or fellow
demonstrators or the long rising pavement

or rain on the hills of Wales, the smear
of light from a bus window, any now
is infinite space, is everything, is whatever
you and it and they are. Now you have it.

*

Today has it all, sunshine,
snow to the north, the lake
frozen over, the Sunday leisure
of friends, a silence like

a seizing up of the megamachine,
a forgetting of towns.
Broken pieces of ice skipped
over ice sing no tunes

but hit one high sweet note
each time they touch the ice,
hold the note to its twittering death
halfway over the lake. Wild geese

are frozen in attitudes, improbably
secure from the fowler. Nothing forages.
Five of us and a happy dog
alone now on the crisp ridges.

The barrowed dead live for us,
we banish fear of raucous change
to this lake, this moorland, this
Wales, dismiss the sly danger

with laughter, love, attention
to now, as given us by all
our senses, the sight, the sound,
the feel, the taste, the ice-sweet smell

of a cerulean winter's day
on water, skin and grass
now we are together and absolute
in this moment of grace.

Gwyn Williams